Book Nook

by Pearl Markovics

Consultant:
Beth Gambro
Reading Specialist
Yorkville, Illinois

Contents

BEARPORT PUBLISHING

New York, New York

Book Nook

Let's rhyme!

This is Tom the **cook**.

Tom stands in a **brook**.

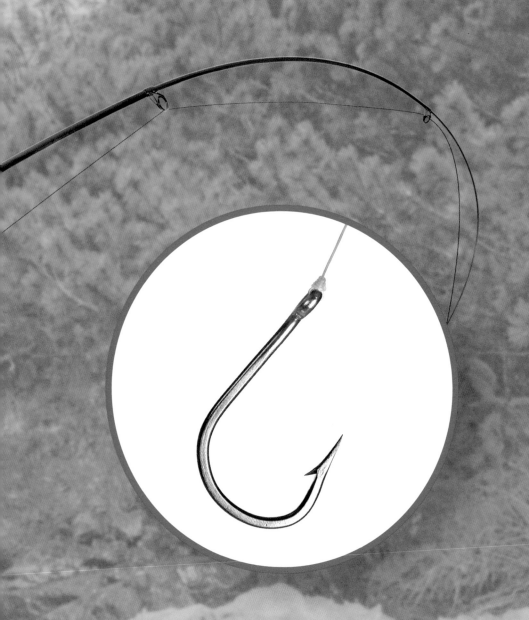

He holds a fishing
pole with a **hook**.

Then, he catches a **book**!

Tom takes a good **look**.

What a surprise!

CHEF
TOM

It is a **cookbook**.

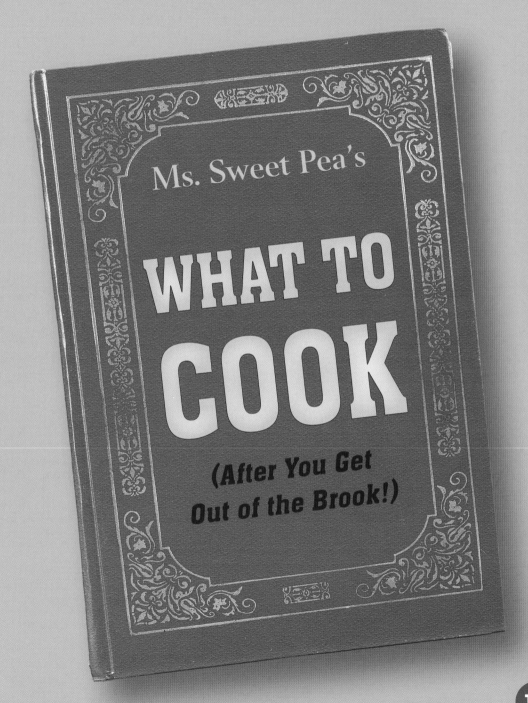

Ms. Sweet Pea's

WHAT TO COOK

(After You Get Out of the Brook!)

The **cook**
puts the **book**
in his **nook**.

Ms. Sweet Pe.

WHAT TO
COOK
(After You Get
Out of the Brook!)

Key Words in the **-ook** Family

book

brook

cook

hook

look

nook

Other **-ook** Words:
crook, rook, shook, took

Index

About the Author

Pearl Markovics enjoys having fun with words.
She especially likes witty wordplay.

Teaching Tips

Before Reading

✔ Introduce rhyming words and the **–ook** word family to readers.

✔ Guide readers on a "picture walk" through the text by asking them to name the things shown.

✔ Discuss book structure by showing children where text will appear consistently on pages. Highlight the supportive pattern of the book.

During Reading

✔ Encourage readers to "read with your finger" and point to each word as it is read. Stop periodically to ask children to point to a specific word in the text.

✔ Reading strategies: When encountering unknown words, prompt readers with encouraging cues such as:

- **Does that word look like a word you already know?**
- **Does it rhyme with another word you have already read?**

After Reading

✔ Write the key words on index cards.

- **Have readers match them to pictures in the book.**

✔ Ask readers to identify their favorite page in the book. Have them read that page aloud.

✔ Choose an **–ook** word. Ask children to pick a word that rhymes with it.

✔ Ask children to create their own rhymes using **–ook** words. Encourage them to use the same pattern found in the book.

Credits: Cover, © Karjalas/Shutterstock, © donatas1205/Shutterstock, © Rose Carson/Shutterstock, and © Daniel Pelaza/Shutterstock; 2–3, © LightField Studios/Shutterstock and © Africa Studios/Shutterstock; 4–5, © LightField Studios/Shutterstock, © Kletr/Shutterstock, © New Africa/Shutterstock, and © Valery Kalantay/Shutterstock; 6–7, © Joe Belanger/Shutterstock and © New Africa/Shutterstock; 8–9, © LightField Studios/Shutterstock, © New Africa/Shutterstock, and © Africa Studios/Shutterstock; 10–11, © LightField Studios/Shutterstock and © Africa Studios/Shutterstock; 12, © LightField Studios/Shutterstock; 13, © Africa Studios/Shutterstock; 14–15, © PinkBlue/Shutterstock, © studiovin/Shutterstock, © Thomas Bethge/Shutterstock, and © Suwatchai Plumruetai/Shutterstock; 16T (L to R), © Africa Studios/Shutterstock, © Valery Kalantay/Shutterstock, and © LightField Studios/Shutterstock; 16B (L to R), © Joe Belanger/Shutterstock, © LightField Studios/Shutterstock, and © studiovin/Shutterstock.

Publisher: Kenn Goin   **Senior Editor**: Joyce Tavolacci   **Creative Director**: Spencer Brinker

Library of Congress Cataloging-in-Publication Data: Names: Markovics, Pearl, author. | Gambro, Beth, consultant. Title: Book nook / by Pearl Markovics; consultant: Beth Gambro, Reading Specialist. Description: New York, New York: Bearport Publishing, [2020] | Series: Read and rhyme: level 2 | Includes index. Identifiers: LCCN 2019007614 (print) | LCCN 2019010565 (ebook) | ISBN 9781642806069 (Ebook) | ISBN 9781642805529 (library) | ISBN 9781642807103 (pbk.) Subjects: LCSH: Readers (Primary) Classification: LCC PE1119 (ebook) | LCC PE1119 .M2853 2020 (print) | DDC 428.6/2–dc23 LC record available at https://lccn.loc.gov/2019007614